The Meal Prep Cookbook & Guide

Learn to Create Tasty Meals That Can Save You Time & Money!

vigor&belle

© 2016

Follow us in Social Media!

Connect with other people, get the latest info, discuss the most recent vigor&belle products or simply show your love for the vigor&belle brand!

Facebook
Connect and become friends with other fans, or comment, discuss the latest posts and releases from vigor&belle.

Instagram
Follow vigor&belle on Instagram for even more healthy recipes, lifestyle and beauty ideas.

Pinterest
Pin, like and comment your favorite vigor&belle recipes and beauty trends.

TABLE OF CONTENTS

Introduction:

If you constantly find yourself rushing from A to B, while crying in vain to find enough time to prepare a meal, you may need a bit of a helping hand. When you have a bit of free time on a Sunday for example, you should think about preparing your meals for the coming week. I've been preparing meals for years, it's something my mother always did, and what I still do.

Meal Preparation Benefits

Meal preparation can make life a lot easier, particularly if you would like to sit down to a homemade dinner, but you simply don't have the time to make one. You should set aside at least a few hours each week in order to prepare your meals, but doing so will save you a lot of time.

How will it save me time?

Preparing meals in one go will save you a lot of time. You will no longer have to stand in front of your oven every night, and you will no longer have a huge pile of dishes to clean. A once a week meal prep 'Session' means you will only have to stand in front of your oven for a few hours once a week. You will also have fewer dishes to wash too, and that can only be a good thing.

Budget Friendly

Meals that you cook from scratch can be very budget friendly, which means you have the potential to save yourself quite a bit of cash. Eating out, ordering take outs, and consuming TV dinners can cost quite a lot of money. We can easily spend $200-$300 dollars a month on TV dinners for the whole family, throw on everything else, and the costs spiral.

When you cook a meal from scratch, chances are you're going to be using the same ingredients again and again. This means that the little pot of mixed herbs you bought last week, can potentially last you for months, if you only use 1 sprinkle per meal. Those fresh vegetables that you buy from your local market won't cost as much as they do in your local store, and they'll stay fresher for longer too.

Another benefit of cooking your own meals is you get to say how big or small your portion sizes are. Let's say for example that one of the recipes in this eBook states that it's suitable for 4 servings. You may decide that you want it to last longer, and thereby reduce the portion sizes slightly to make 6 servings. Imagine, 2 more meals for the price of 4, that's got to be good!

If you don't have a lot of money, but you want to eat a healthy balanced diet that's full of tasty meals, there's nothing stopping you. Ok so the initial outlay you pay out for the ingredients may seem steep, but after a while you won't have to buy so many anymore. You'll also learn where to shop for the cheapest and freshest ingredients too. Budget friendly meals don't have to be full of fat, salt, and sugar, they can be delicious and nutritious, and save you a lot of cash.

Meals Lasting 4-5 Days

The meals that are contained within this book typically keep for 4-5 days, if you store them in the refrigerator. One trick that I've found very useful when making a batch of meals, is to stick a label on the tubs and pots I keep them in. That way if I or one of my family members fancies a meal, they can tell what's in the tub, and when it was cooked.

Meals can last 4-5 days, sometimes a little longer, but you need to be careful when you keep food in the refrigerator. Chicken and pork should be eaten up as quickly as possible, and prawns are just as important too. You should not consume any chicken, pork, or prawn meals that have been in your refrigerator for any more than 5 days.

Freezing Meals

When it comes to freezing meals, you have a real potential to save yourself a lot of time, while also having a delicious meal to hand whenever you want one. You will need to make sure that you don't re-freeze meat or fish (Including prawns) that has previously been frozen. If you're not sure whether the ingredients you're using have been frozen, look at the packaging and product description for details.

Meals are Easy to Reheat

There's no doubt about it, meals that have been frozen or kept in the refrigerator are very easy to re-heat. Some people like to re-heat their meals in the oven, others are happy to use a microwave. Microwaves can be particularly handy as they re-heat food very quickly, but they can also make different foods soggy or dry, plus they can also affect the flavor too.

Whenever you re-heat one of your meals, or even one of the snacks you've made, please make sure they are heated thoroughly each and every time.

Using Single-Serve Containers

Keeping food in single-serve containers is ideal if you often eat by yourself, or you often find yourself wanting something different from the food your family is eating. Single-serve containers can be large enough to fit a good-sized portion, and they can also stack quite nicely in your refrigerator or freezer.

If like me you detest washing up, you can always eat the meal straight out of the container. However, re-heated meals can also be enjoyed on a plate or in a bowl too, whichever takes your fancy.

Include Whole Ingredients

If you want to be as healthy as possible, you can always use whole ingredients in your recipes, such as whole grain bread, flours, and plenty of fresh fruits and vegetables. Please feel free to use fresh tomatoes for example, instead of canned ones. Canned tomatoes are often easier to prepare, and most people are more likely to have them in stock than you have 28 ounces of fresh tomatoes.

Buying the Ingredients You Need

When it comes to shopping for the ingredients you need, you may wonder where to start. Perhaps you're new to cooking meals from scratch, and you're wondering how on earth you're going to store all the ingredients you need. Fear not! There is an easy way for you to go about this. Don't buy every single ingredient that I've mentioned in this eBook, just buy the ingredients you're going to need. Let's say you're thinking of making the Mexican-style beef chili, for this dish you will need:

3 tbsp oil
2 ½ cans kidney beans
2 kg stewing beef
½ tsp oregano
2 onions
1 liter beef stock
2 tbsp chipolte paste
½ tbsp flour
4 cloves garlic
1 tsp cinnamon
25 g ginger
½ tsp cumin

So, when you go out shopping, you need to look for these ingredients, alone. If you want to make another recipe, you'll need to look for those ingredients too, don't forget that bag of flour you bought so you can make meatloaf, can also be used for another dish too. This means that after a while, you're going to have a lot of the ingredients in stock.

If you're serious about preparing meals, please make sure you have all the ingredients you need before you start. Simply make a note of what you need, and how much you need, and then go shopping for it!

Ok that's enough talk, let's take a look at some great recipes!

Breakfast

Why not prepare your breakfasts ahead of time? If you rush around in the mornings trying to get everything done before you leave for work, you may appreciate preparing this important meal beforehand. Some of the recipes can be defrosted in the microwave or in your refrigerator overnight. Others, can be stored in an airtight container, and grabbed as and when you need them.

Make sure you always eat breakfast, it's the most important meal of the day, and it can get your metabolism working faster which is ideal for weight loss.

Meals that can be frozen:

When it comes to freezing your meals, please make sure the food has cooled down first. Food that is still warm when it is placed in a refrigerator or freezer can raise its temperature.

Microwaves can be particularly handy as they re-heat food very quickly, but they can also make different foods soggy or dry, plus they can also affect the flavor too.

Whenever you re-heat one of your meals, please make sure they are heated thoroughly each and every time.

Chocolate & Peanut Butter Oatmeal Protein Cups
Makes: 12

Ingredients
2 tbsp chia seeds
Pinch salt
6 tbsp water
1 tbsp baking powder
3 bananas (Mashed)
2 tbsp cocoa powder
1 cup almond milk
3 cups old fashioned oats
¼ cup peanut butter (Creamy)
1 scoop plant based protein powder (Chocolate flavor)
¼ cup maple syrup
½ tsp vanilla extract

Method:
Preheat your oven to 350 Fahrenheit. Spray your muffin tin with some cooking spray, and set to one side. Add the chia seeds and water to a bowl, and mix well, and set to one side.

Add the mashed bananas to a bowl, and stir in the peanut butter, milk, vanilla, and maple syrup. Add the chia, cocoa powder, salt, protein, baking powder and oats, and stir again. Now spoon the mixture into the muffin tin, making sure you fill them right up to the top. Add to the oven, and bake for 20-25 minutes, or until they are done. Allow to cool. You could also: Freeze in individual containers & microwave as needed, or store in the refrigerator for up to 5 days, & use as needed. Great for: 'On the go' breakfasts, or enjoyed as a healthy snack.

Egg & Ham Cauliflower Muffins
Makes: 6

Ingredients
1 cup cauliflower (Chopped)
Salt & pepper
3 eggs
¾ cup ham (Diced, heavily packed)
1 cup kale (Sliced)

Method:
Preheat the oven to 400 Fahrenheit, and spray a muffin tin with cooking spray, set to one side. Add the cauliflower to a food processor, and blend until it looks like rice. Now add the eggs to a bowl, and place the ham, cauliflower, kale in with them, and season, stir well to combine.

Spoon the mixture into the muffin tin, and add to the oven cook for 20 minutes, or until the eggs are nicely set. Allow to cool.

You could also: Freeze in individual containers & microwave as needed, or store in the refrigerator for up to 5 days, & use as needed.

Great for: 'On the go' breakfasts, or enjoyed as a healthy snack.

Blueberry Granola Carrot Bars
Makes: 8-10

Ingredients
1 ½ cups oat flour
2 tbsp coconut butter (Softened)
½ cup vanilla flavored protein powder
Pinch salt
1/3 cup coconut flour
1/3 cup blueberries
1/3 cup vanilla flavored Greek yogurt
1/3 cup fruit granola
1 tsp vanilla extract
½ tbsp baking powder
1 tbsp cinnamon
1 cup almond milk
1 egg
3 tbsp carrot (Shredded)

Method:
Add all of the dry ingredients to a bowl, and mix well.
Now add the wet ingredients to another bowl, and mix
well. Add the wet ingredients to the dry ones, and stir
well. Now add the mixture to a prepared baking dish,
and cook for 30 minutes, or until the bars are slightly
browned. Allow to cool, and cut into slices.

You could also: Freeze in individual containers &
microwave as needed, or store in the refrigerator for
up to 5 days, & use as needed.

Great for: 'On the go' breakfasts, or enjoyed as a
healthy snack.

Slow Cooker Meals:

Creating slow cooker meals is a great way to save a lot of time and effort. You simply need to do a spot of preparation beforehand, and place everything in a slow cooker. The beauty of these appliances are they're made to be left on for a long time. This means you can cook something overnight, or even when you're at work. Then when the meal/snack is done, you can serve it up, or divide it into portion sizes. When it comes to freezing your meals, please make sure the food has cooled down first. Food that is still warm when it is placed in a refrigerator or freezer can raise its temperature.

Caramelized Cinnamon Rolls
Makes: 8

Ingredients
1 package cinnamon rolls (Chilled)
½ cup brown sugar
4 tbsp butter

Method:
Spray the slow cooker pan with cooking spray, and set to one side. Now add the sugar and butter to a pan, and melt the butter until the mixture is smooth. Add the cinnamon rolls to the slow cooker, and pour the sauce over the top. Add the lid and cook on a high heat for 1 hour. Allow to cool.

You could also: Freeze in individual containers & microwave as needed, or store in the refrigerator for up to 5 days, & use as needed. Great for: 'On the go' breakfasts, or enjoyed as a snack.

Ham & Spinach Breakfast Omelet
Makes: 6 portions

Ingredients
6 eggs
1 cup ham (Diced)
½ tsp salt
1 cup pepper jack cheese (Shredded)
¼ tsp black pepper
1 cup baby spinach
¼ cup milk
1/3 cup mushrooms (Diced)
½ cup Greek yogurt
½ tsp garlic powder
½ tsp thyme
½ tsp onion powder

Method:
Add the salt & pepper, yogurt, onion, garlic, eggs milk
and thyme to a bowl, and mix well. Now add the rest
of the ingredients, and mix again. Spray your slow
cooker pot with cooking spray, and then add the egg
mix into it. Cook on high for 1 ½- 2 hours, or until the
eggs are nicely set. Slice.

You could also: Freeze & microwave as needed, or
store in the refrigerator for up to 5 days, & use as
needed.

Great for: 'On the go' breakfasts.

Creamy Southern-Style Grits
Makes: 4 portions

Ingredients
1 cup stone-ground grits
1 tsp salt
2 cups water
½ cup heavy cream
1 ½ cups milk

Method:
Add the ingredients to a glass bowl or cup that holds no more than 4 cups. Stir well, and then add the bowl or cup to a slow cooker. Now pour enough water into the slow cooker, (Without getting it into the bowl or cup) so that it reaches half way up the cup or bowl. Cook on low for 8 hours, then stir well.

You could also: Allow to cool, and store in the refrigerator for up to 4 days, & use as needed. Alternatively, you could freeze in individual containers, & use as needed.

Banana & Cinnamon French Toast
Makes: 3-4 servings

Ingredients
½ loaf challah bread (Preferably 1 day old, sliced into
½ inch slices)
4 bananas (Sliced)
2 cups whole milk
Pinch salt
4 eggs
1 tsp cinnamon
1 tsp almond extract
5 tsp sugar

Method:
Spray the slow cooker pot with cooking spray, and add
the bread to the pot, ensuring the slices overlap. Now
add the remaining ingredients apart from the bananas
to a bowl, and mix them together well. Once mixed,
pour over the bread, and using a spoon, push the
bread down so it's completely covered by the liquid.
Add the lid, and cook on a low heat for 8 hours. Allow
to cool a little, then cut into portions, and sprinkle the
banana pieces on top.

You could also: Allow to cool, and store in the
refrigerator for up to 4 days, & use as needed.

Great for: 'On the go' breakfasts.

One Pot Meals:

One pot meals not only save on the washing up, but they also show you how you can make a wide range of delicious meals with minimum fuss. There's usually a bit of preparation beforehand, but most of the cooking will take place in 1 pot, or on one baking sheet, and thereby reducing the amount of cleaning up that needs to be done.

Bacon & Egg Breakfast Pizza
Makes: 4 portions

Ingredients
1 pound pizza dough (Room temperature)
Thyme leaves (Minced)
2 tbsp olive oil
Chives (Minced)
5 slices Provolone cheese
Salt & Pepper
1 cup tater tots (Cooked)
3 eggs
4 slices apple wood smoked bacon (Cooked, diced)
3 slices Canadian bacon (Sliced)

Method:
Preheat your oven to 450 Fahrenheit, Add 1 ½ tbsp olive oil to a skillet, and add the pizza dough. Shape the dough into a disk-shape, and stretch it out to create a 12 inch base. Add the rest of the olive oil, and brush it over the dough. Now add the cheese slices, and bacon, then place the tater tots on top, saving room for the eggs.

Place the skillet on a high heat, and cook for 4 minutes, the bottom of the dough should be golden brown. Crack the eggs on top, and season, and place the pizza in the oven for 10-12 minutes, or until the cheese is melted, is bubbling nicely, and the eggs are thoroughly cooked.

Allow to cool and cut into 4-6 slices.

You could also: Freeze & microwave as needed. Allow to cool, and store in the refrigerator for up to 4 days, & use as needed.

Great for: 'On the go' breakfasts.

Healthy One Pot Breakfast
Makes: 4 servings

Ingredients
4-6 slices bacon (Chopped)
1 avocado (Sliced)
2 tbsp avocado oil
4 eggs
½ red onion (Chopped)
3 cups spinach
2 cups butternut squash (Shredded)
4 garlic cloves (Minced)
1 pound sausage

Method:
Brown the bacon in your skillet on a medium heat, and then add the onion and avocado oil. Cook for 3-5 minutes, or until the onion us clear. Now add the sausage and garlic, and cook for about 8-10 minutes, or until the sausage has broken into pieces, and is browned.

Turn the broiler to high, and add the spinach and butternut squash, and cook for another 4-5 minutes. Make some small holes in the mixture, and crack your eggs into them. Broil until the eggs are cooked to your satisfaction, and then allow to cool. Cut into 4 portions.

You could also: Freeze & microwave as needed. Allow to cool, and store in the refrigerator for up to 4 days, & use as needed.

Great for: 'On the go' breakfasts.

Baked Eggs with Cheese & Mushrooms

Makes: 2 portions

Ingredients
1 pound Crimini mushrooms (Sliced)
2 tsp parsley (Chopped)
1 tbsp olive oil
2 tsp Parmesan (Grated)
Salt & pepper
4 eggs

Method:
Preheat your oven to 400 Fahrenheit, and spray a casserole dish with some cooking spray. Now heat the oil in a pan on a high heat, add the mushrooms, and sauté for about 8 minutes, or until all of their liquid has evaporated. Season, and add the mushrooms to the casserole dish.

Break the eggs over the mushrooms, and season, before sprinkling some Parmesan on top. Now add the dish to the oven, and bake for 10 minutes, or until the eggs are done to your satisfaction. Slice into portion sizes.

You could also: Freeze & microwave as needed. Allow to cool, and store in the refrigerator for up to 4-5 days, & use as needed.

Great for: 'On the go' breakfasts.

Breakfasts Prepared for the Whole Week:

Meal preparation can make life a lot easier, particularly if you would like to sit down to a homemade dinner, but you simply don't have the time to make one. You should set aside at least a few hours each week in order to prepare your meals, but doing so will save you a lot of time.

When it comes to freezing meals, you have a real potential to save yourself a lot of time, while also having a delicious meal to hand whenever you want one. You will need to make sure that you don't re-freeze anything that has previously been frozen. If you're not sure whether the ingredients you're using have been frozen, look at the packaging and product description for details.

Healthy Breakfast Burritos
Makes: 6

Ingredients
½ tbsp olive oil
6 tortillas
½ cup onion (Chopped)
2 cups cheddar (Shredded)
1 cup zucchini (Chopped)
½ tsp oregano
1 bell pepper (Chopped)
¼ tsp pepper
1 cup brown lentils (Cooked)
6 eggs

Method:
Heat the oil in a skillet on a medium heat, and add the onion. Cook for about 5 minutes, or until the onion is

clear. Now add the pepper and zucchini, and cook for another 5 minutes. Take the eggs, and add them to a bow, along with the oregano, salt, and pepper, and stir well. Add the eggs along with the lentils to the skillet, and cook for another 4-5 minutes, or until the eggs are done.

Allow the mixture to cool slightly, and then divide it between each of the tortillas. Sprinkle the cheese on top, and roll the tortillas up.

You could also: Freeze in individual containers & microwave as needed. Allow to cool, and store in the refrigerator for up to 6 days, & use as needed.

Great for: 'On the go' breakfasts.

Black Bean & Avocado Tacos

Makes: 2 servings

Ingredients
8 ounces tofu (Firm)
4 corn tortillas
1 cup black beans (Cooked)
¼ cup pomegranate arils
¼ cup red onion (Diced)
1 cup cilantro (Chopped)
1 lime (Sliced)
1 avocado (Sliced)
½ cup salsa
¾ tsp garlic powder
1 tbsp water
½ tsp chili
Pinch sea salt
1 tsp cumin

Method:
Add the beans to a pan, and cook them on a medium heat until they are nice and soft. Reduce the heat, and then set to one side. Add the spices, salsa and salt to a bowl, stir well, and then add sufficient water so you can make a sauce. Set to one side.

Now place the tofu in a skillet, and crumble using a fork. Place on a medium heat, and as soon as the skillet has started to get hot, add 2 tbsp of any oil, and cook the tofu for about 5 minutes, so it's a little brown. Once 5 minutes is up, add the seasoning, and toss it well so it coats the tofu. Cook for about 6-8 minutes, or until you can smell the seasoning. Set to one side.

Add the tortillas to your oven, and heat them on a low heat, this should take 4-5 minutes. Once the tortillas are heated, top them with the tofu, onion, beans, cilantro, avocado, salsa, pomegranate, and lime juice.

You could also: Freeze in individual containers & microwave as needed. Allow to cool, and store in the refrigerator for up to 5 days, & use as needed.

Great for: 'On the go' breakfasts.

Apple Pecan, & Hemp Granola
Makes: 4-5 servings

Ingredients
3 cups rolled oats
½ cup dried apple rings (Chopped)
1 ½ cups pecans (Chopped)
1 tsp vanilla extract
½ cup hemp hearts
1/3 cup honey
1 tsp cinnamon
½ cup apple sauce (Unsweetened)
¼ cup coconut oil (Melted)

Method:
Preheat your oven to 350 Fahrenheit. Add the oats, cinnamon, hemp and pecans to a bowl, and mix well. Now add the rest of the ingredients apart from the apple rings, and stir until the mix is completely coated in the honey and apple sauce. Prepare a baking sheet, and spread the granola out, and then place it in the oven for 15 minutes. Remove from the oven and turn the granola over so it cooks on the other side. Add to the oven for another 15 minutes, and then take it out of the oven, and let it cool completely. Once cooled, add the apple rings, and store in a seal-able container.

You could also: Keep the granola fresh for up to 2 weeks!

Great for: 'On the go' breakfasts.

Grab on the Go:

Meals that can be grabbed 'On the go' will ensure you have at least eaten something at meals times. Those who tend to skip meals for whatever reason, are more likely to become overweight. Do yourself a favor, prepare your 'Grab on the go' meals, so you can grab them when you're on your way to work, or whatever you may be doing.

Blueberry and Coconut Water Breakfast Smoothie
Makes: 1 serving

Ingredients
1 ½ cups blueberries
1 tbsp hemp hearts
1 cup coconut water
¼ tsp coconut extract
½ cup yogurt

Method:
Add all of the ingredients to a blender or smoothie maker, and blend until smooth, pour into a glass, and serve.

You could also: Double up the ingredients, make twice as much, and store in the refrigerator for up to 3 days.

Cherry and Peach Smoothie with Goji Berries
Makes: 1 serving

Ingredients
1 cup cherries (Frozen)
1 tbsp Goji berries
½ cup peach slices (Frozen)
1 ¼ cups almond milk

Method:
Add all of the ingredients to a blender or smoothie maker, and blend until smooth, pour into a glass, and serve.

You could also: Double up the ingredients, make twice as much, and store in the refrigerator for up to 3 days.

Apricot & Walnut Energy Bites
Makes: 3-4

Ingredients
1 cup walnuts
1 tbsp hemp seeds
¼ cup Goji berries
1 tbsp chia seeds
1 tbsp lemon juice
1 zested lemon
4 pre-soaked dates (Pitted)

Method:
Add all the ingredients to a food processor, and blend until they are almost smooth. Add to a baking tray, and freeze for 15 minutes. Remove from the freezer, and cut into 3-4 small bars, or whatever size you fancy. Store in your refrigerator.

You could also: Double up the ingredients, make twice as much, and store in the refrigerator for up to 3 days. You could also freeze in individual containers, defrost overnight or in the microwave, and use as needed.

Great for: Snack time

Lunch

Why not prepare your lunches ahead of time? If you rush around in the mornings trying to get everything done before you leave for work, you may appreciate preparing this important meal beforehand. Some of the recipes can be defrosted in the microwave or in your refrigerator overnight. Others, can be stored in an airtight container, and grabbed as and when you need them.

Make sure you always eat lunch, it can help with concentration levels, which are vital when you're at work. You're likely to have a lot more energy too, and that's never a bad thing.

Meals that can be frozen:

Bacon & Asparagus Quiche
Makes: 6-8 servings

Ingredients
½ tbsp butter
½ cup bacon (Diced, cooked)
½ tbsp olive oil
2 ¾ cups asparagus (Diced, cooked)
1/3 cup onion (Diced)
1 tsp mixed herbs
1 ¼ cups mushrooms (Sliced)
½ tsp salt
1 cup ricotta cheese
½ tsp pepper
1 cup plain yogurt
½ tsp nutmeg
4 eggs

Method:

Preheat your oven to 400 Fahrenheit. Grease a pie pan with butter, and set to one side. Now heat the mushrooms, olive oil and onions in a skillet, and sauté on a medium heat, until the onions are clear. Set to one side. Take a bowl, and add the eggs, cheese, and yogurt, and stir until the mix is nice and creamy. Add the salt, pepper, herbs, and nutmeg, and stir again. Now take the bacon, mushroom mix and asparagus, and fold it gently into the cheese mix. Spoon this mixture into your pie pan, and place in the oven. Cook for 35-40 minutes, or until the eggs are springy, and the quiche is going a little brown around the edges. Allow to cool, and cut into portions.

You could also: Freeze in individual containers & microwave as needed. Allow to cool, and store in the refrigerator for up to 6 days, & use as needed.

Great for: 'On the go' breakfasts.

Grilled Chicken & Roasted Vegetables
Makes: 8 servings

Ingredients
16 ounces quinoa (Cooked)
32 ounces taco lime chicken (Cubed)
16 ounces rice (Cooked)
4 cups cauliflower florets (Roasted)
4 cups asparagus (Chopped, roasted)

Method:
Place the rice, quinoa, cauliflower and asparagus into
a bowl, and mix well. Add the chicken on top, and mix
a little. Divide into 8 portions.

You could also: Freeze in individual containers &
microwave as needed. Allow to cool, and store in the
refrigerator for up to 4 days, & use as needed.

Tuna Salad Sandwich
Makes: 4 servings

Ingredients
10 ounces tuna in water
4 sandwich thins
¼ cup plain yogurt
4 slices provolone cheese
½ tsp lemon juice
½ tsp honey
½ cup carrot (Grated)
¼ tsp garlic powder
¼ tsp dill
¼ cup red onion (Diced)
¼ tsp Dijon mustard
½ tsp parsley (Chopped)
¼ tsp salt

Method:
Add all the ingredients apart from the Provolone, and the sandwich things to a bowl. Mix well, and then spread the mixture into the sandwich things. Sprinkle the cheese on top.

You could also: Freeze in individual containers/bags & microwave as needed. Store in the refrigerator for up to 3 days, & use as needed.

Great for: 'On the go' lunches.

Slow Cooker Meals:

French Onion Soup
Makes: 6 servings

Ingredients
3 pounds onions (Sliced)
6 cups Parmesan cheese (Shredded)
2 tbsp butter (Melted)
2 tsp salt
¼ tsp pepper
¼ cup dry sherry
1 tsp soy sauce
2 tsp garlic (Minced)
1 tsp sugar
4 cups beef broth
1 tsp sugar
2 cups chicken broth
1 bay leaf
5 sprigs thyme

Method:
Add the onions, salt and butter to the slow cooker, and cook on a high heat for 4 hours, or until the onions are a golden brown color. Add the garlic and sherry, and stir well. Now cook for another 10-15 minutes, but with the lid off. Add the broths, sugar, bay leas and thyme, and place the lid back on. Cook for 1 ½ to 2 hours, then take out the bay leaf and thyme, and add the pepper and soy sauce. Stir, and then sprinkle the Parmesan on top.

You could also: Freeze in individual containers & microwave as needed. Allow to cool, and store in the refrigerator for up to 4 days, & use as needed.

Vegetable Soup
Makes: 4 servings

Ingredients
1 tin tomatoes (Chopped)
1 zucchini (Chopped)
2 chicken stock cubes
3 tomatoes (Chopped)
Mixed herbs
1 sweet potato (Peeled, chopped)
½ butternut squash (Peeled, chopped)

Method:
Add all the ingredients to the slow cooker, then add just enough boiling water so that it covers the vegetables. Cook for 5 hours on a high heat.

You could also: Freeze in individual containers & microwave as needed. Allow to cool, and store in the refrigerator for up to 4 days, & use as needed.

Italian-style Chicken and Tomato Soup
Makes: 6 servings

Ingredients
3 chicken breasts (Boneless, skinless)
Pepper
1 onion (Chopped)
½ ts salt
2 garlic cloves (Minced)
1 tbsp basil
1 can coconut milk
2 tbsp Italian seasoning
1 cup chicken broth
14 ounces diced tomatoes

Method:
Add all the ingredients apart from the chicken to your slow cooker. Stir well, and then add your chicken. Cook on a high heat for 4-6 hours, or until the chicken is easy to shred. Take the chicken out of the slow cooker, shred it using two forks, then add it back in and stir well.

You could also: Freeze in individual containers & microwave as needed. Allow to cool, and store in the refrigerator for up to 4 days, & use as needed.

Philly Cheese Steak Sub
Makes: 6 servings

Ingredients
2 pounds round steak
12 slices cheese
½ tsp pepper
6 French rolls
½ tsp garlic powder
32 ounces beef broth
1 onion (Sliced)
1 bell pepper (Sliced)

Method:
Rub the garlic and pepper into the steak, and then place it in the slow cooker. Add the broth, bell pepper and onion, and mix well. Now cook the ingredients on a low heat for 6-7 hours, or until the meat is nice and tender. Preheat your oven to 350 Fahrenheit, and toast the French rolls for a few minutes, until they are going a little crusty. Once the rolls are done, add a few slices of cheese to each of them, and then divide the sandwich mix between the rolls. Place them back in the oven for a few minutes, or until the cheese is melted.

You could also: Freeze in individual containers & microwave as needed. Allow to cool, and store in the refrigerator for up to 4 days, & use as needed.

Great for: 'On the go' lunches.

One Pot Meals:

Zucchini and Lemon Risotto
Makes: 2 servings

Ingredients
50 g butter
2 tbsp crème fraiche
1 onion (Chopped)
50 g Parmesan (Grated)
180 g risotto rice
250 g zucchini (Diced)
1 vegetable stock cube
2 sprigs lemon thyme
juice and zest of 1 lemon

Method:
Add the butter to a skillet, and melt it, then add the onion and fry on a low heat for 5-8 minutes, or until it's soft. Now add the garlic and cook for 1 minute. Add the rice, and stir it well so the butter and onions coat it. Cook for another 2 minutes.

Now take the stock cube, and dissolve in in 1 liter of boiling water. Add 1 ladle of the the stock to the rice, and then add the thyme and lemon juice, and stir. Cook on a medium heat stirring all the time. Do this until all the liquid is absorbed, Now add the zucchini, and stir well, then repeat with another ladle of stock, an continue until you've used all the stock up, and it's all been absorbed, and the rice is creamy. Add the lemon zest crème fraiche and Parmesan.

You could also: Freeze in individual containers & microwave as needed. Allow to cool, and store in the refrigerator for up to 4 days, & use as needed.

Chinese-Style Pork
Makes: 4 servings

Ingredients
400 g Pork fillet
¾ cup scallions (Sliced)
2 ½ cups chicken stock
1 tsp chili flakes
1 tbsp soy sauce
200 g baby leaf greens
2 tsp Chinese spice mix
2 inches ginger (Peeled, finely chopped)

Method:
Add all of the ingredients apart from the green and scallions into a sauce pot, and the lid, and allow to simmer on a medium-high hear. Cook for 8-10 minutes, or until the pork is slightly cooked, and the greens are completely done. Sprinkle the scallions on top.

You could also: Freeze in individual containers & microwave as needed. Allow to cool, and store in the refrigerator for up to 5 days, & use as needed.

Coconut Rice & Salmon
Makes: 6 servings

Ingredients
½ cup cilantro
1 red chili (Seeded, chopped)
3 limes
4 scallions (Thinly sliced)
2 cans coconut milk
2 tsp golden sugar
2 tbsp olive oil
3 tbsp soy sauce
small scoop butter
6 salmon fillets (Skinless)
2 shallots (Chopped)
4 lime leaves
90 g Thai red curry paste
2 ½ cups basmati rice

Method:
Grate the zest of 1 lime, and set to one side. Now add the coconut milk to a bowl, and fill one of the cans with water, and pour this into the bowl. Set to one side. Heat the butter and oil in a skillet on a low heat, and add the shallots. Cook for about 5 minutes, or until the shallots are slightly golden. Add the curry paste, and cook for 1 more minutes.

Remove the skillet from the heat, and then add the cilantro, rice, tsp salt, and lime zest. Mix well, and then pour the coconut milk on top. Stir well, and then add back to the heat, and simmer on a medium heat for a few minutes. Add the lime leaves, stir, and simmer for 5 more minutes.

Stir the rice, then place the salmon on top of the rice. Cover, and simmer on a low heat for up to 20 minutes, or until the salmon is cooked.. Now squeeze the juice out of 2 of the limes, and add the sugar and soy sauce to it, and mix well. Add the scallions, cilantro and chili, and chop the remaining lime into wedges.

Take the rice and fish off the heat, and set to one side for 5 minutes. After 5 minutes, make your servings. Add 1/3 of the salad to each portion/pot add the coconut rice, place a salmon fillet on top, and sprinkle the dressing on. Add a lime wedge on top of that.

You could also: Freeze in individual containers & microwave as needed. Allow to cool, and store in the refrigerator for up to 3 days, & use as needed.

Prepare on Sunday for the Whole Week:

Quinoa and Kale Salad with Almonds and Orange Dressing

Makes: 3 servings

Ingredients
½ tbsp olive oil
¼ cup whole almonds (Roasted, salted, chopped)
½ onion (Diced)
¼ cup dates (Pitted)
Salt
½ bunch kale (Sliced)
¼ cup red quinoa
½ garlic clove (Crushed)
Juice of ½ Mandarin orange
Salt & pepper
Juice of ¼ lime
1 tsp maple syrup

Method:
Heat the oil in a skillet, and add the onion, and a bit of salt. Cook on a medium heat for 20 minutes, or until the onion is caramelized. Set to one side. Add the garlic and quinoa to a sauce pot, and cook on a medium heat for 1 minute to toast to quinoa. Add ½ tsp salt and 1 cup water, and allow to boil. Now place the lid on the pot. And cook for 12-15 minutes, then turn the heat off, but leave the lid on for 5 more minutes, then fluff the quinoa with a fork.

Add the lime and orange juice to a bowl, and mix them together well. Now add the oil and syrup, and mix again. Add 2 tbsp of this dressing to the quinoa, and mix well. Now add the kale to the quinoa, along with the onions, and mix well. Add half of the remaining dressing and mix well again. Add the almonds and dates, season, and add the rest of the dressing if you wish.

You could also: Store in your refrigerator for up to 5 days.

Great for: 'On the go' lunches.

Red Falafel with Salad
Makes: 5 servings

Ingredients
1 cup red lentils (Soaked)
Cooking spray
2 cups parsley leaves
½ tsp baking soda
2 cups cilantro leaves
1 tsp coriander
5 cloves garlic
1 tsp cumin
2 tbsp chick pea flour
1 red onion (Chopped)
1 tsp salt
1 Serrano pepper (Chopped)
1 ½ tbsp olive oil
1 ½ tbsp tahini paste

For the dressing:
1/3 cup tahini paste
Salt & pepper
Juice of 1 lemon
½ tsp paprika
3 tbsp water
¼ cup parsley (Minced)
1 clove garlic (Grated)

For the salad:
3 cups kale (Shredded)
Salt & pepper
3 carrots (Grated into ribbons)
1 tbsp lemon juice
¼ cup red onion (Sliced)
3 tbsp olive oil

Method:

Add the lentils to a food processor and pulse until they are ground. Now add the pepper, cilantro, parsley, garlic, and onion to the lentils, and pulse again. Add the olive oil, salt, pepper, tahini and spices, and blend until you have a smooth-ish mixture. Add the chick pea powder and baking soda, and mix well. If you have too much liquid, add some more flour. Place the mixture into your refrigerator for a least 30 minutes.

Preheat your oven to 375 Fahrenheit. Now add the tahini paste, water and lemon juice to a bowl and mix until they're creamy. Add the parsley, paprika, and garlic and season. Set to one side. Now add all the salad ingredients to a bowl, and mix them well. Take the falafel mix out the refrigerator, and take out 2 tbsp worth at a time, and make them into a ball shape using your hands. Place the ball onto a lined baking sheet, and do the same with the rest of the mixture. Spray the falafels with cooking spray, and add to your oven. Bake for 20 minutes, or until they are golden brown. Divide the salad between tubs, add a spoonful of the dressing on top, and then 3-4 falafels on top of that.

You could also: Store in your refrigerator for up to 5 days.

Great for: 'On the go' lunches.

Sweet Potato Wraps With Onions & Pesto
Makes: 4-5 servings

Ingredients
1 ½ sweet potatoes (Cubed)
Olive oil
¼ cup pesto
1/3 cup Parmesan (Grated)
1 ½ Portobello mushrooms (Sliced)
1 pint small tomatoes (Halved)
4-5 wraps
1 yellow onion (Peeled, sliced)

Method:
Preheat your oven to 400 Fahrenheit, and line 2
baking sheets. Add the tomatoes, mushrooms and
sweet potatoes to the sheet, and drizzle the olive oil
over them, and season. Toss well, and then spread
them out. Add to the oven and cook for 35-45
minutes, or until the mushrooms and tomatoes are
soft, and the potatoes are a little brown.

Heat a skillet, and add the onions and 1 tbsp olive oil.
Cook on a medium heat for until the onions are soft.
Add some water to deglaze the plan, if the skillet is
getting dry. Set to one side.

Now place the wraps in a skillet, and warm them for
about 10 seconds. Spread 2 tsp pesto on each wrap,
and add some mushrooms, potatoes, tomatoes and
onions, along with some Parmesan to each wrap.
Close the wrap.

You could also: Store in your refrigerator for up to 5
days. Add to your freezer, and defrost as needed.
Great for: 'On the go' lunches.

Parmesan Chicken With Roasted Romaine Lettuce

Makes: 4 servings

Ingredients

4 chicken breasts (Boneless, skinless)
1 lemon (Chopped into wedges)
Salt & pepper
4 anchovy fillets (Chopped)
½ cup Parmesan (Grated)
2 hearts romaine lettuce (Chopped lengthwise)
½ cup breadcrumbs
2 cloves garlic (Chopped)
3 tbsp extra virgin olive oil
2 tbsp parsley

Method:

Preheat your oven to 450 Fahrenheit, and then line a baking sheet with foil. Season the chicken, and add it to the sheet. Now add the rest of the ingredients apart from the anchovies, and lemon wedges 1 tbsp oil, and 1 garlic clove to a bowl, and mix well. Take the mixture in your hands, and pat it gently onto the chicken. Add to the oven and cook for 10 minutes, or until the crumbs are golden brown.

Now drizzle the remaining oil over the lettuce, and sprinkle the rest of the garlic on top. Season, and then add the chicken to the baking sheet, Cook for about 10 minutes, or until the chicken is thoroughly cooked, and the lettuce has started to go a little brown at the edges. Top with the anchovies, and place the lemon wedges around the edges.

Grab on the Go:

Middle-Eastern Wrap

Makes: 1 serving

Ingredients
½ cup romaine lettuce (Shredded)
3 dolmas
¼ cup cucumber (Chopped)
1 wrap
¼ cup tomato (Chopped)
1/8 tsp garlic powder
¼ cup plain yogurt
1 tbsp feta cheese

Method:
Add the garlic, feta, cucumber, yogurt, lettuce and tomato to a bowl, and mix well. Spread this mixture onto the wrap, and add the dolmas on top. Roll up the wrap.

You could also: Store in your refrigerator for up to 5 days. Add to your freezer, and defrost as needed.

Turkey Pastrami Sandwich
Makes: 1 serving

Ingredients
2 slices turkey pastrami
1 slice rye bread (Halved)
5 apple slices (Thin)
1 slice cheese
2 tbsp sauerkraut

Method:
Place all of the ingredients onto one half of the bread, add the other slice on top.

You could also: Store in your refrigerator for up to 5 days. Add to your freezer in individual containers, and defrost as needed.

Curried Chicken Pita Pockets
Makes: 4 servings

Ingredients
6 tbsp plain yogurt
2 cups sprouts
¼ cup mayonnaise
4 pita breads
1 tbsp curry powder
¼ cup almonds (Sliced, toasted)
2 cups chicken breast (Cubed)
½ cup dried cranberries
1 pear (Diced)
1 celery stalk (Diced)

Method:
Add the mayonnaise, curry powder and yogurt to a bowl, and mix well. Now add the rest of the ingredients apart from the sprouts. Mix well, and then fill the pita pockets with the chicken mix. Add the sprouts on top, and close the pockets as much as you can.

You could also: Store in your refrigerator for up to 4 days. Add to your freezer in individual containers, and defrost as needed.

Dinner

Why not prepare your dinners ahead of time? If you rush around at lunch time trying to meet deadlines while wishing you had time to eat, you may appreciate preparing this important meal beforehand. Some of the recipes can be defrosted in the microwave or in your refrigerator overnight. Others, can be stored in an airtight container, and grabbed as and when you need them.

Make sure you always eat dinner, it's a hugely important meal, and one that can help your body to get the energy and sustenance it needs after a long hard day.

Meals that can be frozen:

Chicken Tortilla Soup
Serves: 4

Ingredients
4 corn tortillas (Cut into strips)
¾ cup cheddar (Shredded)
1 tbsp extra virgin olive oil
½ cup cilantro (Chopped)
1 pound chicken breast (Skinless, boneless, diced)
2 tbsp lime juice
3 cups pepper & onion mix
15 ounces diced tomatoes with chilies
1 tbsp cumin
28 ounces chicken broth

Method:
Preheat your oven to 350 Fahrenheit. Now spread the tortillas onto your baking sheet, and cook for about 10

minutes, or until they are turning a little brown. Add the chicken to a Dutch oven and cook on a medium high heat until it starts to brown, this should take about 4 minutes. Once the chicken is starting to brown, place it on a plate, and set to one side.

Add the peppers & onions to the Dutch oven, along with the cumin, and stir well. Cook until the onions are a little brown. Add the lime juice, pepper, broth and tomatoes, and mix well. Cook until the pepper is tender. Now add the chicken again, and stir well, cook for 1 minute, or until it's heated thoroughly. Remove the soup from the heat, stir in the cilantro, and top off with the tortillas and cheese.

You could also: Store in your refrigerator for up to 4 days. Add to your freezer in individual containers, and defrost as needed.

Sweet Mustard Salmon & Vegetables

Makes: 3-4 servings

Ingredients
4 cups kale (Chopped)
3 tbsp sweet mustard
1 tbsp whole grain mustard
2 tbsp parsley leaves (Chopped)
2 cups cherry tomatoes
1 tbsp honey
Salt & black pepper
4 salmon fillets
1 tbsp soy sauce

Method:
Preheat your oven to 400 Fahrenheit. Now Spray a baking sheet with some cooking oil. Add the mustard to a bowls, along with the soy sauce, and honey and set to one side.

Add the tomatoes and kale to the baking sheet, and pour the olive oil over the top. Season with the salt and pepper and place the salmon on the top of the vegetables. Brush each piece of salmon with mustard, and add the salmon to the oven. Cook for 18 minutes, ensuring you brush the fish with a bit more mustard every 6 or so minutes.

You could also: Store in your refrigerator for up to 4 days. Add to your freezer in individual containers, and defrost as needed.

Cheddar Stuffed Meat Loaves
Makes: 4 servings

Ingredients
1 pound ground beef
1/8 tsp chipolte pepper
½ cup onion (Chopped)
½ cup cheddar cheese (Shredded)
1/3 cup breadcrumbs
¼ tsp ground pepper
1 egg
¼ tsp salt
6 tbsp ketchup
1 tsp cumin
2 tsp chili powder

Method:
Preheat your oven to 400 Fahrenheit, and spray some cooking spray on a baking sheet. Add the onion, breadcrumbs, beef, 2 tbsp ketchup, salt, pepper, onion, chili powder and cumin to a bowl, and stir well. Now divide this mix into quarters, and place them on the baking sheet. Make a line down the middle of the meat loaves and fill the hole with cheese. Close the hole as much as you can.

Now take the chipolte, and leftover ketchup, and place them in a bowl, mix well, and then spoon this over each of the loaves. Add to the oven, and bake for about 30 minutes.

Chicken with Sweet Potatoes
Makes: 4 servings

Ingredients
2 tbsp Dijon mustard
1 red onion (Chopped into wedges)
2 tbsp thyme
2 sweet potatoes (Peeled, sliced)
2 tbsp extra virgin olive oil
1 ½ pounds chicken thighs (No skin, with bones)
½ tsp salt
½ tsp black pepper

Method:
Turn your oven on to 450 Fahrenheit, and add the baking sheet to the oven. Take a bowl, and in it add the mustard, 1/4 tsp salt, 1/4 tsp pepper, and 1 tbsp oil. Mix well, and then coat the chicken with the sauce.

Add the potatoes and onion to a different bowl, mix well, and add the rest of the oil, salt, and pepper. Now take the baking sheet out of the oven, and place the vegetables on it. Add the chicken on top, and then cook for 40-45 minutes, or until the vegetables are a little brown, and the chicken is cooked thoroughly.

You could also: Store in your refrigerator for up to 5 days. Add to your freezer in individual containers, and defrost as needed.

Buffalo Chicken Pizza
Makes: 6-8 servings

Ingredients
1 tube pizza crust (Chilled)
½ tsp oregano
1 cup Buffalo wing sauce
2 tbsp butter
2 pounds chicken breasts (Skinless, boneless, cubed)
1 ½ cups cheese (Shredded)
½ tsp salt
½ tsp pepper
½ tsp garlic
½ tsp chili powder
1 ½ cups mozzarella cheese (Shredded)

Method:
Unroll the pizza crust, and place it on a greased baking sheet. Add to your oven, and bake for 7 minutes at 400 Fahrenheit. Once 7 minutes is up, brush the base with 3 tbsp of the Buffalo sauce. Take a bowl, add both cheeses, mix well, and then sprinkle 1/3 of it onto the crust.

Take a skillet, and add the salt, pepper, chili, and garlic, and stir. Add the chicken, and cook thoroughly. Now add the rest of the Buffalo sauce, and mix well. Cook for another 5 minutes. Once 5minutes is up, spoon this mixture over the pizza, and sprinkle the oregano and the rest of the cheese on top.

Add to the oven, and bake for about 20 minutes, or until the crust has started to go golden brown. Serve.

You could also: Store in your refrigerator for up to 5 days. Add to your freezer in individual containers, and defrost as needed.

Great for 'On the go' dinners.

Slow Cooker Meals:

<u>Meatloaf</u>
Makes: 4-6 servings

<u>Ingredients</u>
2 eggs (Beaten)
3 garlic cloves (Minced)
2/3 cup milk
1 onion (Minced)
¼ cup ketchup
2 celery stalks (Diced)
2 tsp Dijon mustard
Salt & pepper
1 tsp hot sauce
½ tsp marjoram
2/3 pound lean beef (Ground)
½ tsp thyme
1/3 pound pork (Ground)
¼ cup parsley (Chopped)
3 slices bread (Made into breadcrumbs)

For the sauce:
1 cup ketchup
1 tbsp cayenne pepper
½ cup brown sugar
3 tbsp Dijon mustard
1/3 cup Worcestershire sauce
¼ cup red wine

<u>Method:</u>
Add the sauce ingredients to a bowl and whisk them well. Set to one side. Now add the eggs, hot sauce, mustard and milk to another bowl, mix well, add the breadcrumbs, and allow to soak for 5-6 minutes.

Take another bowl, and in it add the meat, salt, pepper, thyme, sugar and marjoram, mix well, and add the parsley, onion, celery and salt, and mix again. Add the breadcrumb mix to the meat mix, and mix them together well using your hands. Shape the mix into a loaf shape, and then spray your slow cooker with some cooking spray. Place the loaf into the slow cooker, and brush ¼ of the sauce over the sides and top.

Cook the meatloaf for 1 hour on a high heat, then reduce the heat to low, and cook for 3-4 hours, or until the meat is cooked thoroughly. Brush the meatloaf with some more sauce, and then allow the meatloaf to stand for 10 minutes, before slicing.

You could also: Store in your refrigerator for up to 4 days. Add to your freezer in individual containers, and defrost as needed.

Great for: 'On the go' dinners.

Low Fat Sweet & Sour Chicken
Makes: 4 portions

Ingredients
2 pounds chicken breasts (Skinless, boneless)
2 cups cooked rice (For serving)
1 cup corn starch
2 sweet bell peppers (Deseeded, sliced)
¼ tsp black pepper
1 cup pineapple chunks
Cooking oil
2 tbsp corn starch
3 tbsp water
1/3 cup soy sauce
½ tsp ginger (Minced)
¼ cup chicken broth
2 cloves garlic (Minced)
3 tbsp ketchup
¼ tsp sesame oil
3 tbsp honey
2 tsp oyster sauce
1 ½ tbsp rice vinegar
2 tsp oyster sauce

Method:
Add the black pepper, chicken and corn starch to a resealable bag, and shake well, so the chicken is coated. Now heat the oil in a skillet on a medium heat, and add the chicken. Brown for about 2 minutes on each side, and then add the chicken to a slow cooker. Now take a bowl, and in it add the oyster sauce, broth, soy sauce, sesame oil, ginger, garlic, ketchup, honey and broth. Mix well, and pour this over the chicken. Cook for 3-4 hours on a low heat.

Add the water and corn starch to a bowl, and mix well, then add this to the slow cooker, and stir. Now add the peppers and pineapples, stir again, and cook on a high heat for 15-20 minutes, and spoon over the rice.

You could also: Store in your refrigerator for up to 4 days. Add to your freezer in individual containers, and defrost as needed.

Balsamic Beef Pot Roast
Makes: 4-6 servings

Ingredients
1 beef chuck roast (Boneless)
3 tbsp water
Salt & pepper
3 tbsp corn starch
2 tbsp olive oil
2 bay leaves
1 pound baby carrots (Chopped)
½ tsp sage
3 celery stalks (Chopped)
1 tsp thyme
1 onion (Sliced)
3 garlic cloves (Minced)
½ cup balsamic vinegar
14 ½ ounces beef broth
1 cup tomato juice

Method:
Heat the oil in a pan on a medium heat. Add the beef, and sear on each side. Take the beef out the pan, and add it to your slow cooker. Add the celery, onions and carrots on top of the beef. Now take a bowl, and in it place the broth, thyme, garlic, vinegar, tomato juice and sage, and then pour this into your slow cooker. Add the bay leaves on top, and then cook for 10 hours on a low heat.

Once the beef is cooked, set it and the vegetables to one side. Now spoon the fat off the top of the liquid, and then pour it into a pan. Now add the corn starch and water to a bowl, and mix it well, then pour this into the pan. Cook for about 2 minutes, or until the sauce starts to thicken. Pour the sauce over the meat.

You could also: Freeze in individual containers & microwave as needed, or store in the refrigerator for up to 5 days, & use as needed.

One Pot Meals:

<u>Mexican-Style Beef Chili</u>
Makes: 7-8 servings

<u>Ingredients</u>
3 tbsp oil
2 ½ cans kidney beans
2 kg stewing beef
½ tsp oregano
2 onions (Sliced)
1 liter beef stock
2 tbsp chipolte paste
½ tbsp flour
4 cloves garlic (Crushed)
1 tsp cinnamon
25 g ginger (Grated)
½ tsp cumin

<u>Method:</u>
Heat some oil in a skillet, and then add the meat a little at a time. Add more oil as needed. Once the meat is browned, set to one side. Now add ½ tbsp oil, along with the onions, and cook for 5-6 minutes, or until the onions are starting to brown a little. Add the chipolte, flour, cinnamon cumin, ginger, and garlic, and cook for 2-3 minutes. Then pour in the stock while stirring, and then add the oregano and tomatoes. Season, and allow to simmer for 10 minutes.

Add the beef, and cover, and simmer for about 1 ½ hours, or until it's tender. Take the lid off, add the beans, and simmer for 10-15 minutes.

You could also: Freeze in individual containers & microwave as needed, or store in the refrigerator for up to 5 days, & use as needed.

Pork Stew & Corn Dumplings
Makes: 6 servings

Ingredients
900g Pork shoulder (Sliced into 4cm pieces)
2 cans black beans
2 tbsp oil
2 red peppers (Deseeded, chopped)
2 onions (Chopped)
400 g sweet potatoes (Peeled, chopped)
2 celery sticks (Chopped)
Bunch scallions (Chopped)
3 bay leaves
2 red chilies (Peeled, sliced)
2 tsp oregano
Juice and zest of 2 oranges
1 tbsp cumin
3 tbsp red wine vinegar
1 tbsp coriander
2 tbsp muscovado sugar
1 tbsp allspice
1 tbsp cocoa powder
1 stock cube
2 cans chopped tomatoes

For the dumplings:
100 g butter (Cold, chopped)
1 egg (Beaten)
¾ cup self rising flour
75 ml buttermilk
140 g corn meal
Small can sweet corn
½ tsp baking soda

Method:
Seal the pork pieces in a skillet so they're brown on all sides, then set to one side. Add ¾ of the onion, oregano, and the bay leaves to the skillet, and fry for a few minutes, or until the onion is soft. Now add the spices, and cook for 1 more minute. Place the pork back in the skillet, and break the stock cube over the top. Add the sugar, cocoa, zest and juice of 1 orange, 2 tbsp vinegar, and ¾ of the chili to the skillet. Simmer, then cover and allow to bubble for one hour. Take the remaining chili, and mix it with the onions, red wine vinegar, scallions, and the remaining orange zest and juice. Place in the refrigerator to chill.

Now add the red peppers, and sweet potatoes to the stew, and stir well, and simmer for 30 minutes. Now add the butter and flour together, and rub it with your hands to make a crumb-like texture. Add the sweetcorn, corn meal and baking soda. Add the buttermilk, and the egg apart from 1 tbsp, and make a dough. Season, and create 12 balls, add more corn meal, and then brush the balls with the remaining egg.

Heat your oven to 400 Fahrenheit, and add the beans to the stew. Season, and place half the dumplings on top of the stew. Add the remaining dumplings to a baking sheet. Add the stew (Uncovered) and dumplings to the oven, and cook for 20-25 minutes, or until the dumplings have risen, and are golden brown.

You could also: Freeze in individual containers & microwave as needed, or store in the refrigerator for up to 5 days, & use as needed.

Spanish-Style Rice & Prawns
Makes: 4 servings

Ingredients
1 onion (Sliced)
200g prawns (Raw, peeled, defrosted)
1 red pepper (Deseeded, sliced)
1 can chopped tomatoes
1 green pepper (Deseeded, sliced)
1 cup basmati rice
50 g chorizo (Sliced)
1 tbsp olive oil
500ml water (Boiling)
2 cloves garlic (Sliced)

Method:
Add the onions, garlic, peppers and chorizo to a skillet on a high heat, and cook for 3 minutes. Add the tomatoes and rice, and add the water, cover, and cook for 12 minutes. Stir the rice, add the prawns and a little more water if you need to. Cook for 1 more minute, or until the prawns are pink.

You could also: Store in the refrigerator for up to 4 days, & use as needed.

Prepare on Sunday for the Whole Week:

Jalapeño Sausage & Vegetable Stir Fry
Makes: 6 servings

Ingredients
1 onion (Diced)
Pinch salt
1 clove garlic (Minced)
¼ tsp red pepper flakes
1 tbsp olive oil
1 tsp onion & herb blend
4 Jalapeño chicken sausages (Chopped)
1 can tomatoes
1 red bell pepper (Deseeded, sliced)
1 head broccoli florets
1 orange bell pepper (Deseeded, sliced)
1 yellow bell pepper (Deseeded, sliced)

Method:
Add the onion, garlic and a bit of olive oil to a skillet and sauté on a medium heat, until the vegetables start to release their aroma. Add the sausage, and cook for a few more minutes. Add the broccoli, and peppers, and cook for 3 more minutes, before adding the tomatoes. Stir well, and season. Cook for 5 more minutes, and stir again.

You could also: Freeze in individual containers & microwave as needed, or store in the refrigerator for up to 5 days, & use as needed.

Turkey Chili

Makes: 8 servings

Ingredients
2 pounds turkey (Ground)
1/8 tsp cayenne pepper
1 onion (Chopped)
2 tsp oregano
5 cloves garlic (Minced)
3 tbsp chili powder
1 tbsp olive oil
1 packet sweetener
28 ounces crushed tomatoes
Pinch pepper
15 ounces petite diced tomatoes
1 ½ tsp salt
3 tbsp tomato paste
2 jalapeños (Chopped)
½ tsp hot sauce
1 green bell pepper (Chopped)
15 ounces kidney beans
1 red bell pepper (Chopped)

Method:
Add some olive oil to a pot, and stir in the garlic and onion, and cook for 3 minutes. Now add the turkey, and cook until it's browned, this should take about 5 minutes on a medium heat. Add the remaining ingredients, and cook on a low heat for 1 hour.

You could also: Freeze in individual containers & microwave as needed, or store in the refrigerator for up to 4 days, & use as needed.

Fried Cauliflower Rice

Makes: 4 servings

Ingredients
1 head cauliflower (Chopped)
2 tbsp green onions (Chopped)
1 yellow onion (Chopped)
½ cup peas (Frozen)
Pinch red pepper flakes
½ cup carrots (Chopped)
1/8 tsp ginger
2 eggs (Beaten)
1 tbsp light brown sugar
1 tbsp sesame oil
¼ cup soy sauce

Method:
Add the cauliflower florets to a food processor, and pulse until it starts to look like rice. Set to one side. Now heat a skillet on a medium heat, and add some sesame oil. Now add the carrots, onion and peas, and sauté for 2 minutes, or until tender. Take a bowl, and in it add the soy sauce, sugar, red pepper flakes, and ginger, stir well, and set to one side. Add the vegetable mixture to one side of the skillet, and add the eggs, scramble for a few minutes, or until they are thoroughly cooked. Add the rice, and pour the soy sauce over it. Cook for another 2-3 minutes, or until the cauliflower is soft. Sprinkle the green onions on top.

You could also: Freeze in individual containers & microwave as needed, or store in the refrigerator for up to 4 days, & use as needed.

Lemon Chicken & Potato Bake
Makes: 4 servings

Ingredients
4 chicken legs
12 ounces green beans
24 ounces potatoes
2 tbsp herb and lemon seasoning
½ cup olive oil
1 tbsp black pepper
Juice of 2 lemons
1 tbsp salt
2 tbsp basil
2 tbsp oregano

Method:
Preheat your oven to 425 Fahrenheit, and then prepare a sided baking sheet. Add the chicken to the baking sheet, and set to one side. Now place the potatoes, seasoning, olive oil, salt, 1/2 the lemon juice, pepper, basil and oregano in a bowl, and mix until the potatoes are coated in the sauce. Now pour 3/4 of the mix over the chicken, and then drizzle the rest of the lemon juice over it too.

Add to the oven, and bake for 30 minutes, then shake the baking sheet so the potatoes loosen slightly. Place back in the oven, and cook for another 15 minutes. Now add the green beans to the leftover oil, and toss well. Take the chicken out the oven, pour the green beans over it, and then return the chicken to the oven, and cook for 10-15 minutes, or until the beans are cooked to your satisfaction. Please make sure the chicken is thoroughly cooked.

You could also: Freeze in individual containers & microwave as needed, or store in the refrigerator for up to 4 days, & use as needed.

Grab on the Go:

<u>Chicken Fajitas</u>
Makes: 3 Servings

<u>Ingredients</u>
1 pound chicken (Skinless, boneless)
½ red onion (Chopped)
Juice of 2 limes
2 bell peppers (Chopped)
1 tsp salt
1 tbsp coconut oil (Melted)
2 tsp chili powder
¼ tsp black pepper
1 tsp garlic powder
¼ tsp coriander
½ tsp paprika
1 tsp cumin

<u>Method:</u>
Add the juice of 1 ½ limes to a bowl, along with ¼ tsp cumin, ½ tsp salt, 1.4 tsp chili, and ¼ tsp cinnamon. Mix well, and then add the chicken, and cover the chicken with the mix. Place in the refrigerator for at least 6 hours.

Once 6 hours has passed, preheat your oven to 450 Fahrenheit. Remove the chicken from your refrigerator, and remove the excess sauce. Cut the chicken into strips, and then add it to a bowl with the leftover spices, coconut oil, and onion. Mix well.

Spread this mixture onto a baking sheet, and cook for 10 minutes, then broil for another 5 minutes, or until the peppers go a little black around the edges. Remove from the oven, and ensure the chicken is thoroughly cooked. Add the rest of the lime juice, and serve.

You could also: Freeze in individual containers & microwave as needed, or store in the refrigerator for up to 4 days, & use as needed.

Great for: 'On the go' dinners.

Sriracha & Barbecue Kabobs
Makes: 4 servings

Ingredients
1 pound chicken thighs (Diced)
2 tbsp maple syrup
2 bell peppers (Diced)
¼ tsp black pepper
1 onion (Diced)
1 ½ tsp paprika
2 zucchini (Chopped)
½ tsp onion powder
2 cups mushrooms (Halved)
1 tbsp soy sauce
1 tbsp olive oil
1 tsp Worcestershire sauce
2 garlic cloves (Chopped)
1 tsp apple cider vinegar
¼ cup sriracha
3 ounces tomato paste

Method:
Add all the ingredients apart from the chicken, zucchini, pepper, and mushrooms to a blender or food processor. Blend well until the sauce is smooth. Now place half the sauce in a bowl and add the chicken to it. Cover the chicken with the sauce, and then place the bowl in your refrigerator for about 3 hours.

Once 3 hours is up, preheat your oven to 375 Fahrenheit. Place the chicken pieces, along with the pepper, zucchini and mushroom onto some kabob sticks, and add them to a baking sheet. Now cook the kabobs in the oven for about 15 minutes, turn them over so they can cook on the other side, for another 15 minutes. Serve with the remaining sauce for dipping.

You could also: Freeze in individual containers & microwave as needed, or store in the refrigerator for up to 4 days, & use as needed.

Great for: 'On the go' dinners.

Snacks

Why not prepare your snacks ahead of time? If you rush around in the evenings trying to get your meals fixed before you can even think about relaxing, you may appreciate preparing this these important snacks beforehand. Some of the recipes can be defrosted in the microwave or in your refrigerator overnight. Others, can be stored in an airtight container, and grabbed as and when you need them.

You don't have to consume snacks if you would rather not eat between meals, but if you do, please make sure you try to eat more healthy snacks.

Meals that can be frozen:

Strawberry and Apricot Tart
Makes: 6-8 servings

Ingredients
1 ½ cups whole wheat flour
1 ½ cups strawberries (Sliced)
½ cup almond flour
1 ½ cups apricots (Sliced)
7 tbsp granulated sugar
1/3 cup strawberry preserve
1 tsp lemon zest
1 tsp vanilla extract
½ tsp salt
3 egg yolks
6 tbsp butter (Unsalted, sliced)
Pinch salt

Method:
Preheat your oven, and spray a round pan with cooking spray.

Add the flours, zest and salt to a bowl, along with 6 tbsp of sugar. Work the butter and flour together, and then make a well in the center. Add the egg and vanilla, and mix them very well. Now crumble the mix using your hands, until it almost looks like wet sand. Measure out 1 cup of this mixture, and set that to one side.

Now place the rest of the mixture into the pan, and spread it across the bottom evenly. Spread the preserve over the crust, and then overlap a ring of apricots around the inner edge. Fill the middle with strawberries that overlap, and then sprinkle the rest of the sugar over the fruit. Then do the same with the cupful of mixture. Place into the oven, and cook for 30 minutes, then lower the temperature to 325 Fahrenheit. Bake for 30-35 minutes, or until the fruits are bubbling. Allow to cool before cutting.

You could also: Freeze in individual containers & microwave as needed, or store in the refrigerator for up to 5 days, & use as needed.

Great for: 'One the go' snacks.

Coconut Cake
Makes: 4-6 servings

Ingredients
2 cups all-purpose flour
½ cup coconut for sprinkling
1 ½ tsp baking powder
2 cups confectioners sugar
½ tsp salt
1 cup butter (Unsalted, room temperature)
1 tsp coconut extract
2 cups sugar
1 cube butter (Room temperature)
5 eggs
8 ounces cream cheese
1 cup milk
Sweetened coconut for frosting

Method:
Preheat your oven to 325 Fahrenheit, and spray a cake pan with cooking spray. Add the flour, salt, and baking powder to a bowl, and mix well. In another bowl, add the sugar and cream, and mix them well, then add the eggs, and mix again.

Take another bowl, and add the coconut extract, and shredded coconut, mix well, and add the flour mix to it, and mix again. Pour this batter into the cake pan, and bake for 1 hour, or until the cake is golden brown. Allow to cool.

Now add the cream cheese and butter to a bowl, and mix thoroughly. Add the confectioners sugar, and coconut extract. Mix until the ingredients are fluffy, and then spread this over the cake. Sprinkle the remaining coconut on top.

You could also: Freeze in individual containers & microwave as needed, or store in the refrigerator for up to 6 days, & use as needed.

Great for: 'On the go' snacks.

Pineapple with Honey Pistachios
Makes: 4 servings

Ingredients
½ cup brown sugar
2 tbsp mint leaves (Shredded)
½ cup orange juice
1/3 cup pistachios (Unsalted, chopped)
3 tbsp honey
¼ cup crème fraiche
1 pineapple (Cored, peeled, chopped into wedges)

Method:
Preheat your oven to 450 Fahrenheit, and line a baking sheet. Add the sugar, orange juice and honey to a bowl, and mix well. Add the pineapple, and mix it until it's covered in the orange and honey. Set to one side for 10 minutes.

Once 10 minutes is up, place the pineapple on the baking sheet, with any flat side facing down. Add to the oven, and occasionally brush the pineapple with the marinade, while cooking for 15 minutes.

Once 15 minutes is up, drizzle the rest of the marinade over the top, and then allow it to cool. Add to tubs or containers, and spoon some crème fraiche on the side, and sprinkle the mint and pistachios over the top.

You could also: Freeze in individual containers & microwave as needed, or store in the refrigerator for up to 6 days, & use as needed.

Great for: 'On the go' snacks.

Slow cooker:

Pumpkin Pie Cake
Makes: 1 cake

Ingredients:
½ cup butter (Unsalted, softened)
½ tsp salt
2 cups brown sugar
1/8 tsp cloves (Ground)
1 ½ tsp baking soda
3 eggs
½ tsp pumpkin spice
15 ounces pumpkin
½ tsp cinnamon
1 ½ cups all purpose flour
1 ½ tsp baking powder

Method:
Line your slow cooker with the sling provided, and
spray it with cooking oil. Add the butter and sugar to a
bowl, and mix it together well. Add the eggs one at a
time, and stir until they are completely combined.
Add the pumpkin, and beat well.

Take a bowl, and add the baking soda, salt, spices, and
baking powder, and mix well. Add the flour a little at a
time, stirring as you do. Now pour this mix into the
slow cook on a high heat for 3 hours, or until a
toothpick that's been inserted into it comes out clean.
Remove the cake from the slow cooker, and allow to
cool.

You could also: Freeze in individual containers &
microwave as needed, or store in the refrigerator for

up to 6 days, & use as needed. Great for: 'One the go' snacks.

Prepare on Sunday for the Whole Week:

Mixed Fruit & Yogurt Bites
Makes: 12 servings

Ingredients
12 wonton wrappers
1/3 cup kiwi fruit (Peeled, chopped)
1/3 cup Granola
1/3 cup blueberries (Halved)
1/3 cup Strawberry (Halved)

Method:
Preheat your oven to 375 Fahrenheit. Spray a muffin tin with cooking spray, and add the wonton wrappers. Press them firmly into the tin, and place the tin in the oven for 6-8 minutes, or until the wrappers are starting to turn golden brown. Set to one side.

Add the fruit to a bowl, and mix well, then add the granola, and mix again. Spoon this mix into the wonton wrappers.

You could also: Freeze in individual containers & microwave as needed, or store in the refrigerator for up to 4 days, & use as needed.

Great for: 'One the go' snacks.

Sweet Potato Curry Chips
Makes: 4 servings

Ingredients
1 medium size sweet potato (Skin on, sliced)
Salt
1 tbsp extra virgin olive oil
½ tsp curry powder

Method:
Preheat your oven to 275 Fahrenheit. Add the potatoes and oil to a bowl, and mix well. Now place the potatoes on a cookie sheet, ensuring they do not overlap. Bake for 40 minutes, then using some tongs, turn them over, and bake for another 40 minutes, or until the edges are crispy and brown. Sprinkle the curry powder over the chips.

You could also: Store in a sealed container for up to 3 days, & use as needed.

Great for: 'One the go' snacks.

Frozen Trail Mix Bars
Makes: 6-8 bars

Ingredients
2 cups Greek yogurt
½ cup chocolate chips
1 ½ cups mixed fruit (Chopped)
¾ cup granola
½ cup almonds (Chopped)

Method:
Add all the ingredients to a bowl, and mix thoroughly.
Now line a deep baking sheet with foil, and pour the
mixture onto it. Cover with some plastic wrapping,
and place in your freezer for 2-3 hours, or until frozen.
Once frozen, remove from the freezer, and allow to
defrost for about 5 minutes. Slice the block into bars,
and then place them back in the freezer

You could also: Freeze in individual containers & use
as needed.

Great for: 'One the go' snacks.

Grab on the Go:

<u>Quinoa & Pumpkin Parmesan Fritters</u>
Makes: 14 servings

<u>Ingredients</u>
1 cup quinoa (Cooked)
Salt & Pepper
½ cup Parmesan (Grated)
¼ cup breadcrumbs
1 egg
1 cup pumpkin puree

<u>Method:</u>
Line a baking sheet, and then add the quinoa to a bowl. Now add the breadcrumbs, salt, pepper, pumpkin, egg, and cheese, and stir well. Scoop the mix with your hands, and then make them onto ¼ inch thick patties. Add the patties to the prepared baking sheet, and set to one side.

Now heat 1 tbsp vegetable oil in a skillet on a medium-high heat. Add 2 fritters, and cook until they are browned on each side.

You could also: Freeze in individual containers & microwave as needed, or store in the refrigerator for up to 4 days, & use as needed.

Great for: 'On the go' snacks.

Green Bean Fries

Makes: 6 servings

Ingredients

1 cup breadcrumbs
2 eggs (Beaten)
½ cup Parmesan (Grated)
Pinch cayenne pepper
½ cup all-purpose flour
Salt & pepper
1 ½ pounds green beans (Trimmed)

Method:

Preheat your oven to 425 Fahrenheit, and spray a baking sheet with cooking spray. Add the breadcrumbs, cayenne pepper, Parmesan and salt & pepper to a bowl, and mix well. Set to one side.

Using a few at a time, dip the beans into the flour, then the eggs, and lastly the breadcrumb mix. Now place these on a baking sheet, making sure none of them overlap.

Cook for 10-12 minutes, or until they are a little brown and crispy.

You could also: Freeze in individual containers & microwave as needed, or store in the refrigerator for up to 6 days, & use as needed.

Great for: 'On the go' snacks

Asparagus Fries
Makes: 4 servings

Ingredients
1 cup breadcrumbs
2 eggs (Beaten)
½ cup Parmesan (Grated)
Pinch cayenne pepper
½ cup all-purpose flour
Salt & pepper
1 pound Asparagus (Trimmed)

Method:
Preheat your oven to 425 Fahrenheit, and spray a baking sheet with cooking spray. Add the breadcrumbs, cayenne pepper, Parmesan and salt & pepper to a bowl, and mix well. Set to one side.

Using a few at a time, dip the asparagus into the flour, then the eggs, and lastly the breadcrumb mix. Now place these on a baking sheet, making sure none of them overlap.

Cook for 10-12 minutes, or until they are a little brown and crispy.

You could also: Freeze in individual containers & microwave as needed, or store in the refrigerator for up to 6 days, & use as needed.

Great for: 'On the go' snacks

Conclusion

As you can see, you can create a wide range of tasty meals and snacks, even if you want to prepare them in advance. Meal preparation can make life a lot easier, particularly if you would like to sit down to a homemade dinner, but you simply don't have the time to make one. You will have to set aside at least a few hours each week in order to prepare your meals, but doing so will save you a lot of time.

Get used to preparing food this way

At first, preparing meals this way may seem a bit strange. Perhaps you're used to making a meal, and then eating it right away. There's nothing wrong with doing this, but as you know, it's not always very convenient. Make life easy on yourself, and get used to preparing food ahead of time. Trust me, it will make your life so much easier, and after a while it will become second nature.

Allocate parts of your freezer and refrigerator to prepared meals

This is easier than it sounds if you plan to use a lot of the same size tubs. Tubs of the same size can stack neatly and nicely in your freezer and refrigerator, without taking up too much room. Before you decide to put a week's worth of meals in the freezer, please make sure you have enough room in there. You may need to have an 'Eat up' before you start, but that can be fun.

Allocate a shelf or two in your freezer and refrigerator, so you know where prepared meals and snacks live, and so does everyone else. Oh, and don't forget to label the meals and snacks, so you know what they are, and when they're made. This will make life so much easier when you're looking for something to eat.

Preparing for the day ahead

Get used to grabbing the meals and defrosting them in the morning. Leave them in the refrigerator if they've been in the freezer, and 'Ping' them in the microwave when you get home. Alternatively, you may want to defrost the meals the night before, and take them to work with you.

It's entirely up to you what you do, just get used to planning ahead, and you won't have a mad rush when it comes to choosing what to eat.

As a side note, some people like to reheat their meals from frozen. This can take a little longer than if the meals were defrosted, but it won't take too much longer. You should be aware that some of the meals will cook a little more while you're reheating them, so you may find you need to adjust the cooking times a little if you want to avoid this.

What tubs should I use?

That's a very good question, and it's entirely up to you. I like to use tubs that can be stacked on top of each other, and will fit nicely in my refrigerator or freezer. You should ideally use tubs that can be sealed properly, are microwave-safe, or oven-safe, and can be washed and used again. Not only are reusable tubs better for the environment, but they will also work out cheaper in the long-run too.

If you like to make soup, a great way to store it is to spoon it into a freezer bag, and lay it flat on a baking sheet, before placing it in the freezer. Once the soup is frozen, you can remove the baking sheet, and the soups will be just fine as they are. Alternatively, you may want to place a freezer bag into a cup or mug, fill it with a portion of soup, seal the bag, remove it from the cup, and place it in your freezer. You'll have to make sure you keep the bag upright so the soup doesn't spill out before it freezes. This is a great way to save a bit of room in your freezer.

Experiment with the recipes

As soon as you've started to feel a little more confident in the kitchen, you may want to think about experimenting with the recipes found in this book. You don't have to stick to them if you don't want to, you can always substitute one ingredient for another. You may also want to try your own recipes, and see how they work out, making a note of any you particularly like.

Cooking isn't just about following recipes, it's also about seeing what works, and what you can make with the ingredients you have. Get used to preparing meals, and enjoy it!

Thank You

Before you go, we would like to say a warm "THANK YOU" on behalf of the Vigor & Belle family! We started this brand to help our customers live healthier, more vibrant lives and we hope that this book has served you in many ways.

If you enjoyed this book, then we'd like to ask you for a favor!

Please take a moment and leave a review for this book after you turn the page.

This feedback is crucial for us to continue to help you to live a healthier, happier and more vibrant lifestyle! If you loved this book, we would love to hear from you!

Live Healthy & Stay Beautiful,

The vigor&belle Family

Made in the USA
Middletown, DE
22 December 2016